Charleston

SOUTH CAROLINA

A PHOTOGRAPHIC PORTRAIT

PHOTOGRAPY BY

Rick Rhodes

NARRATIVE BY

Aleigh Acerni

TWIN LIGHTS PUBLISHERS, ROCKPORT, MASSACHUSETTS

Copyright © 2014 by
Twin Lights Publishers, Inc.

All rights reserved. No part of this book may be reproduced in any form without written permission of the copyright owners. All images in this book have been reproduced with the knowledge and prior consent of the artists concerned and no responsibility is accepted by producer, publisher, or printer for any infringement of copyright or otherwise, arising from the contents of this publication. Every effort has been made to ensure that credits accurately comply with information supplied.

First published in the United States of America by:

Twin Lights Publishers, Inc.
51 Broadway
Rockport, Massachusetts 01966
Telephone: (978) 546-7398
www.twinlightspub.com

ISBN: 978-1-934907-33-7

10 9 8 7 6 5 4 3 2

(opposite)
Ashley River

(frontispiece)
Angel Oak

(jacket front)
Pineapple Fountain

(jacket back)
Lowcountry Marsh

Book design by:
SYP Design & Production, Inc.
www.sypdesign.com

Printed in China

Founded by English colonists in 1670, Charleston is a modern port city with an Old World sensibility. Evidence of its historical importance can be found around every corner. Patriots fought—and won—the first decisive battle of the Revolutionary War here. Cadets from the city's military college, The Citadel, were among the soldiers who fired the first shots of the Civil War across Charleston Harbor.

Over the centuries, the city has withstood devastating fires and earthquakes, been battered by hurricanes and bruised by war, and yet has managed to preserve its beautiful and historically significant architecture. Graceful, elaborate antebellum homes with large porches overlook the now peaceful harbor, where the picturesque Ashley and Cooper rivers intersect to join the Atlantic Ocean.

Church steeples still dominate the Charleston skyline, earning it the nickname "Holy City." A stroll down a Charleston sidewalk reveals the city's timeless charm, from cobblestone streets to colorful window boxes fragrant with jasmine and manicured gardens that hide behind wrought iron gates. Imposing live oaks, decked with Spanish moss, offer shade during Lowcountry summers.

But the true soul of the city is its people, and Charlestonians continue to define Southern hospitality. From its stunning architecture to its renowned cuisine and cultural heritage, global influences permeate the city. Beautiful beaches, sprawling plantations, and scenic salt marshes beg to be explored. This is Charleston.

Palmetto Tree *(opposite)*

South Carolina's state tree has a prominent role on the state flag and is an important part of Charleston's landscape. The tree's flexible trunk made it the perfect building material for the walls of Fort Moultrie. Palmetto logs were also used to help defend the city during the Revolutionary War.

Hampton Park Gazebo *(opposite)*

One of two remaining structures from the Charleston Exposition, this gazebo has been moved from its original location and rebuilt twice. The grounds have served as a plantation, a horse race course, a POW camp and Civil War cemetery, and a zoo.

Fountain at Hampton Park *(top)*

One of the city's largest parks, Hampton Park lies on the site of the Charleston Exposition (formally named South Carolina Inter-State and West Indian Exposition), held here from December 1, 1901 to June 20, 1902. This pond and fountain, although not in their original design, are remnants of the event.

Moss-draped Trees *(bottom)*

Following the Exposition, the Olmsted Brothers landscaping firm from Brookline, Massachusetts was hired to design Hampton Park, which has evolved many times over the years but still includes graceful trees, a trail, and an old rose collection. The park is a popular location for weddings and family reunions.

Riverfront View *(above)*

Considered one of the finest examples of Georgian-Palladian architecture in the United States, Drayton Hall, built from 1738 to 1747, has been preserved as close to original condition as possible. In the early 20th century, the Drayton family planted this allée of azaleas along the riverfront landscape.

African-American Cemetery *(left)*

The earliest mention of this sacred space as a burying ground dates from about 1790, making it one of the oldest African-American cemeteries in the nation still in use. The wrought-iron memorial gate was designed by renowned Charleston blacksmith Philip Simmons.

Drayton Hall *(opposite)*

The grounds at Drayton Hall are one of the most significant, undisturbed historic landscapes in America, including this Victorian reflecting pool along the lawn-front façade. It is the only plantation on the Ashley River to survive the American Revolution, Civil War, earthquake of 1886, and many hurricanes intact.

Live Oaks *(opposite, top and bottom)*

Moss-draped oak trees form a natural corridor to Boone Hall Plantation, founded in 1681 by Englishman Major John Boone. Eight miles from downtown Charleston, it is one of the nation's oldest working plantations, producing crops for more than three centuries.

Boone Hall Plantation *(above)*

It isn't known when John Boone built the original house on the plantation, but the current mansion at Boone Hall was built in 1936 by Canadian ambassador Thomas Stone. The first floor of the house is open to the public; guided tours, presented year round, begin on the front porch.

Historic Slave Cabins

Nine of the original twenty-seven slave cabins still exist along a slave street on the grounds at Boone Hall Plantation. Dating from approximately 1790, the structures are unusual, as most slave cabins were built using wood, while these are constructed of bricks that were made on the property.

Slave Cabin *(above)*

At Boone Hall Plantation, slaves who lived in cabins like this one produced millions of bricks each year. In addition to many houses in downtown Charleston, bricks from the plantation were used to construct the German Friendly Society Kitchen on Archdale Street, St. Stephen's Episcopal Church, and St. John's Lutheran Church.

Cotton *(right)*

Indigo and cotton were Boone Hall Plantation's original primary crops; a cotton gin building on the grounds likely dates to the 1850s, although the cotton gin has been lost. Today the building serves as a restaurant and gift shop.

Pineapple Fountain *(above)*

Pineapples are the international symbol of hospitality, and the iconic Pineapple Fountain is a highlight of Waterfront Park, one of the peninsula's most popular destinations. Offering views of Charleston Harbor, the park was completed in 1990 and includes a splash fountain, pier, and several wooden swings.

Charles Towne Landing *(opposite, top)*

This historic site, on a marshy point just off the Ashley River, marks the location where, in 1670, a group of British settlers founded the Carolina colony. Visitors can tour *Adventure*, a 17th-century replica ship, watch as cannons are fired, explore 80 acres of gardens, and interact with hands-on exhibits.

Founders Hall *(opposite, bottom)*

The park, first opened in the 1970s, received a full renovation and was reopened in 2006. Built to complement the nearby Visitors Center, it is comprised of 9,000 square feet of interior space and a 1,800-square-foot porch. This popular wedding site offers a private courtyard and sprawling lawn.

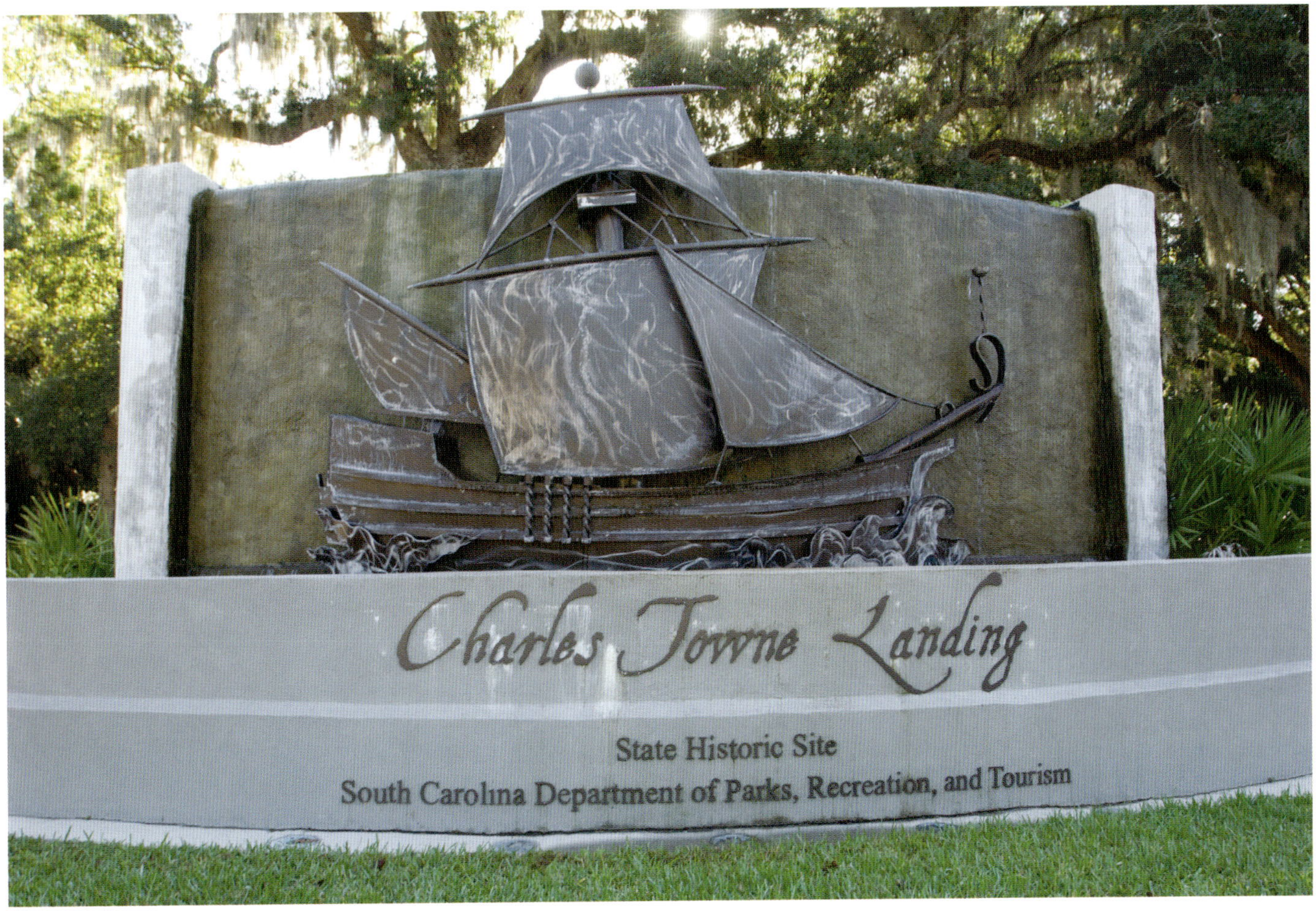
Charles Towne Landing
State Historic Site
South Carolina Department of Parks, Recreation, and Tourism

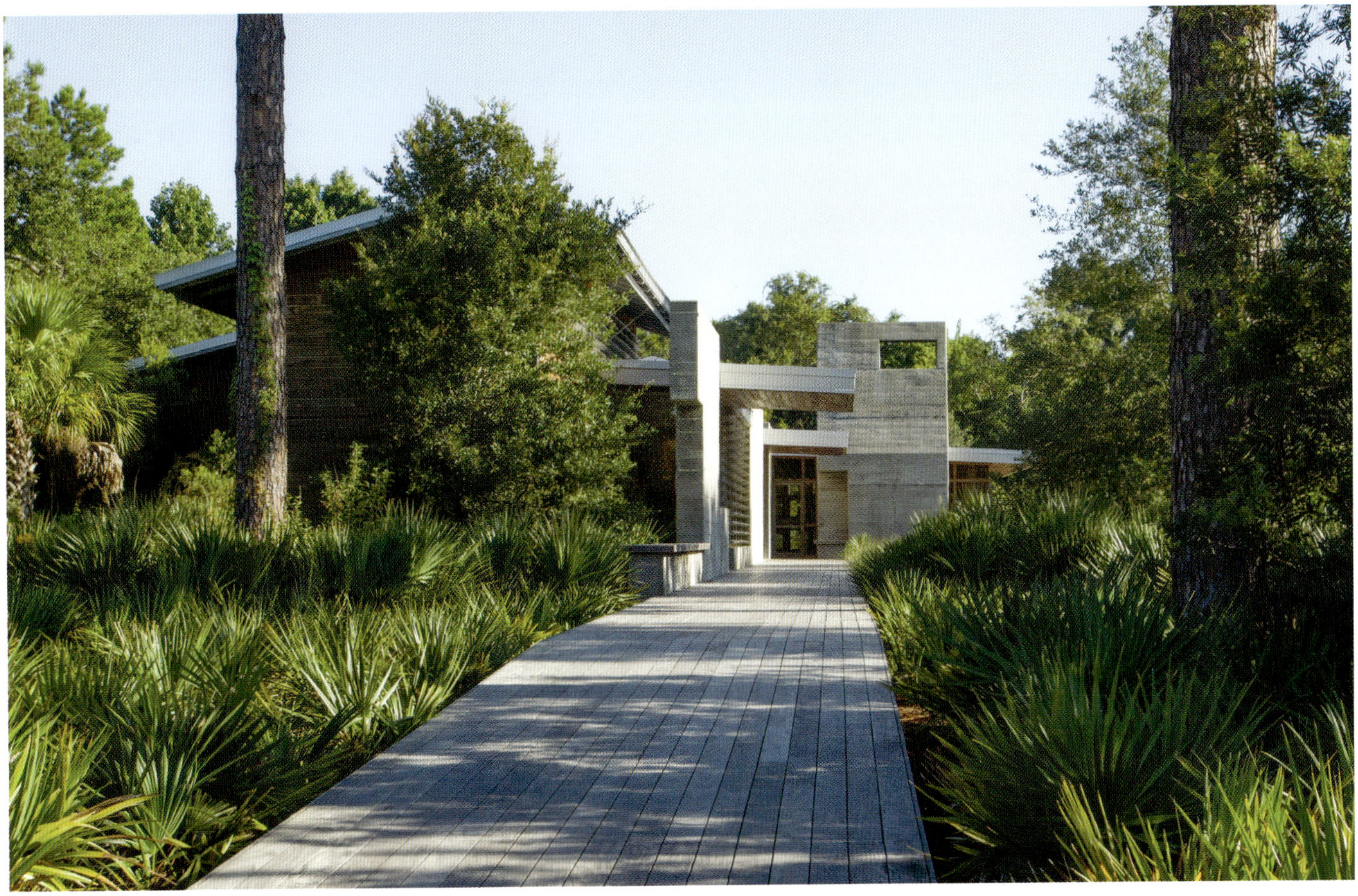

Lowcountry Marsh

Charleston County has the greatest share of salt marshes in South Carolina. In these beautiful wetlands that interlace throughout the Lowcountry, cord grass, salt marsh cord grass, and marram grass are the dominant plant life. Fish that thrive here include croaker, drum, flounder, kingfish, menhaden, mullet, and spot.

Port of Charleston *(top)*

The nation's fourth-busiest, the Port of Charleston benefits from geography (it's halfway between Miami and New York City), the deepest water in the South Atlantic, and a large natural harbor. Every hour, it handles more than $3 million in cargo.

Castle Pinckney *(bottom)*

During a visit in 1791, George Washington ordered a fort built on strategically located Shutes Folly, a small island in Charleston Harbor. The horseshoe-shaped fort was the first seized by Confederate forces. Long neglected and not open to the public, it was purchased in 2011 by Sons of Confederate Veterans.

Arthur Ravenel Jr. Bridge *(opposite)*

When it opened in 2005, the imposing 3.5-mile Arthur Ravenel Jr. Bridge was the longest cable-stayed bridge in North America. Connecting the Charleston peninsula and Mount Pleasant with a span of 1,546 feet, the eight-lane bridge includes a bike and pedestrian lane.

Shem Creek

The 2.5-mile deepwater tidal creek in Mount Pleasant is home to a large shrimping fleet and a popular place to watch for dolphins. At the mouth of the creek, the Crab Bank Seabird Sanctuary, a sandpit island, is one of only nine active seabird-nesting sites in the state of South Carolina.

Charlotte Street Park *(top)*

Opened in June 2013 and designed by graduate students from the Savannah College of Art and Design, Charleston's Charlotte Street Park honors Irish Americans who helped found, develop, and govern the city. The park's centerpiece is a raised, 24-by-30-foot carved granite map of Ireland.

Mayor's Gate *(bottom)*

Designed by landscape architect Sheila Wertimer, the Mayor's Gate is a homage to Charleston mayors with Irish ancestry, including mayors John P. Grace (the city's first Irish-American mayor) and Joe Riley (mayor of Charleston since 1975), who are both represented in the historical text at the base of the gate.

Sullivan's Island Lighthouse *(opposite)*

The last major lighthouse built by the federal government, the lighthouse on Sullivan's Island has several unusual features, including its unique triangular shape, air conditioning, and elevator—although the final ascent to the lantern room requires scaling a 25-foot ladder. It is not open to the public.

Sullivan's Island *(top and bottom)*

Originally called Moultrieville, Sullivan's Island was renamed for Captain Florence O'Sullivan. There are few rental properties and no hotels or other lodging establishments here. Instead, about 2,000 full- and part-time residents make their homes on this barrier island at the mouth of the Charleston Harbor.

Vendue Wharf

This oversized pier is one of the hallmarks of Waterfront Park. Residents and visitors gather here to walk, fish, picnic, or swing on the family-sized "Charleston chairs" that hang under the covered walkway. The pier offers some of the best views of the Ravenel Bridge, Castle Pinckney, and Fort Sumter.

Splash Fountain *(opposite, top)*

At the end of Vendue Range, marking the northern entrance to Waterfront Park, the splash fountain is a favorite place for kids—of all ages—to play and cool off, especially during hot Lowcountry summers. Staying dry? Waterfront Park also has free Wi-Fi.

Waterfront Park *(opposite, bottom)*

A grassy, palmetto-lined lawn lies parallel to the riverfront in the award-winning linear park, recognized by the American Society of Landscape Architects as a distinguished landscape architecture project that "contributes significantly to the public realm of the community in which it is located."

Path at Waterfront Park *(above)*

Benches sit under a canopy of oak trees along Waterfront Park's shady path, which links the splash fountain at the northern end to the North Adger's Wharf, a pier that was rebuilt on the footprint of the original 17th-century pier using native palmetto trees and the original granite.

USS Yorktown

Originally *Bon Homme Richard* but renamed in honor of the ship sunk at the Battle of Midway, *Yorktown* was the tenth aircraft carrier to serve in the US Navy. The centerpiece of the Patriots Point Naval and Maritime Museum, it earned 11 battle stars for service during World War II.

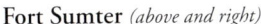

Fort Sumter *(above and right)*

A property of the National Park Service, the five-sided, three-story masonry sea fort in Charleston Harbor was built after the War of 1812 and named for South Carolina Revolutionary War patriot Thomas Sumter. Confederate artillery fired the shots at the fort on April 12, 1861 that launched the American Civil War.

Moultrie Statue

Overlooking the harbor from White Point Garden, this eight-foot-tall statue of General William Moultrie sits atop a seven-foot-tall pedestal and commemorates his leadership during the Revolutionary War, when he led a garrison of 400 men to victory over a British attempt to seize Charles Towne.

Fort Moultrie *(top and bottom)*

The first fort on Sullivan's Island, Fort Moultrie was not yet completed when British forces attacked it on June 28, 1776. General Moultrie, the fort's namesake, is credited with designing a flag based on the uniforms and badges of the fort's guards. That flag later became the South Carolina state flag.

John C. Calhoun Monument *(opposite)*

This statue at Marion Square on the corner of Meeting and King streets memorializes John C. Calhoun, a South Carolina native who served as Secretary of War, U.S. Senator, and was the seventh vice president of the United States. It is the second Calhoun statue to stand on this spot.

Confederate Defenders Monument *(above)*

Honoring the Confederate defense of Charleston during the Civil War, this allegorical statue in White Point Garden was completed in 1931. The male figure is the defending warrior, holding a sword and shield, and the female figure, holding a garland of laurel and pointing toward the sea, represents the city.

Charleston Marsh *(pages 34 – 35)*

Salt marshes, the transitional areas between land and water, are more than just beautiful—they also act as filters to remove sediments and toxins from the water and are among the most productive ecosystems on the planet. Charleston County has some of the largest numbers of salt marshes in the state.

Washington Square *(above and left)*

Washington Square, at the corner of Broad and Meeting streets, was the city's first public park. Shaded with live oaks, it is home to a statue of George Washington and a miniature replica of the Washington Monument in Washington, D.C., which was designed by Charleston native and architect Robert Mills.

William Pitt's Statue *(opposite)*

Commemorating William Pitt, champion of the American colonies against the Stamp Act, Joseph Wilton's 1770 sculpture depicted Pitt in a toga holding the Magna Carta with one hand and the other extending upward. Damaged by British during the siege of Charleston, it was moved to Washington Square in 1891.

Fountain Walk (*above and opposite*)

A commercial hub along Aquarium Wharf, Fountain Walk overlooks the Cooper River and the Ravenel Bridge; it's home to restaurants, shops, a yoga studio, and the American Military Museum. Charter boat tours launch from the attached dock.

Rainbow Row *(top)*

Built in the 1800s, the string of 14 residences began to draw attention in the early 1900s when Dorothy Pocher Legge purchased homes on East Bay Street and painted them in a Caribbean color scheme. Neighbors followed her lead, and now the townhomes are one of the most famous landmarks in the city.

Cobblestone Street *(bottom)*

Few of Charleston's cobblestone streets remain—many of them were replaced in the 19th century—but stumbling upon one of these streets feels like stepping back in time. Purportedly paved with ballast from colonial ships, the Preservation Society of Charleston has worked hard to preserve these streets.

Dock Street Theatre *(opposite)*

The first building in America built just for theatrical performances, the original Dock Street Theatre opened in 1736 on the corner of Church and Dock streets. The current building, which was rebuilt as the Planter's Hotel after a fire, was renovated in 2010, receiving state-of-the-art lighting and sound updates.

Charleston City Market

Charleston City Market was built between 1804 and the 1830s and originally housed meat, vegetable, and fish markets. One of the oldest public markets in the country, today it contains shops selling everything from traditional sweetgrass baskets to clothing, artwork, jewelry, and other items.

Market Hall

The Greek Revival-style Market Hall, designed by Edward Brickell White, was completed in 1841 after the Masonic Hall on the site was destroyed by fire. Today, it houses the Confederate Museum, operated by the Daughters of the Confederacy, and displays Confederate memorabilia including flags, uniforms, and swords.

Judicial Center

The Ernest Hollings Judicial Center on Meeting Street is named for the former governor and senator. A modern addition to the complex, which also includes the Charleston Federal Courthouse and Post Office & Judicial Building, it is set off by a courtyard and fountain.

City Hall *(above and right)*

A carriage tour passes by City Hall through "Four Corners of Law," an intersection bordered by four buildings that represent the four arms of the law: ecclesiastical, state, federal, and municipal. The building was home to the First Bank of the United States before becoming City Hall in 1818.

Avery Research Center

Located on the College of Charleston campus, the Avery Research Center collects, preserves, and shares African-American heritage in Charleston and the Lowcountry. An on-site museum offers free, guided tours and research opportunities, and presents public lectures, discussions, and workshops.

The Pirate House *(above)*

Dainty window boxes belie the history of this Charleston landmark, but the heavy anchor mounted on the wall offers a clue. This is the Pirate House on Church Street, once a tavern and reportedly a popular hangout of pirates and other unsavory characters during the 1700s.

Pirates Courtyard *(right)*

Between the Pirate House and St. Phillips Church Cemetery, a narrow passage leads to Pirates Courtyard, a shady patio with a large, ivy-covered fountain, which was once the preferred tavern entrance of pirates seeking to avoid arrest. Its most famous visitor may have been Edward Teach—otherwise known as Blackbeard.

Wentworth Mansion

(above, left, and opposite)

For 360-degree sunset views of the city and harbor, climb to the cupola of the Wentworth Mansion, built in 1886 as the home of a wealthy cotton merchant. Restored and converted into a boutique hotel in 1998, it includes award-winning restaurant, Circa 1886, along with a full-service spa housed in the mansion's former stables.

Old Marine Hospital

One of only eight remaining marine hospitals built before the Civil War, construction of this National Historic Landmark was completed in 1834. Its history includes being used as a free school for black children, an orphanage, and now, administrative offices for the Housing Authority of Charleston.

Exchange Building

The Old Exchange and Provost Dungeon served as the backdrop for many important historical events, from the first reading of the Declaration of Independence in South Carolina to serving as the meeting place for the ratification of the new state constitution.

South Carolina Society Hall *(top)*

Today one of the South's finest venues for events and wedding receptions, the South Carolina Society Hall was built between 1799 and 1804 and originally served as a meeting place and a school for orphans.

Charleston County Courthouse *(bottom)*

The beautiful Neoclassical-style courthouse is the second building to exist on this site; the original, which was built as the Capitol building for the colony of South Carolina, burned in 1788. It has housed court and county government functions since its completion in 1792.

U.S. Custom House *(opposite)*

This imposing structure on East Bay Street, built in the late 1800s as a home for the Custom Service as a result of Charleston's thriving port, was saved from demolition in the 1960s. It is a rare example of an historical building in Charleston that is still used for its original intended purpose.

Kahal Kadosh Beth Elohim
(above and left)

Founded in 1749, the striking Kahal Kadosh Beth Elohim is built in the Greek revival style. It is the second-oldest synagogue building in the United States—and the oldest in continuous use. An iron fence and menorahs are all that remain from the original structure.

First Baptist Church

The earliest Baptist church in the South, First Baptist was organized under the sponsorship of the First Baptist Church of Boston. The building was designed by architect Robert Mills and completed in 1822. It has survived damage done by the Civil War and the earthquake of 1886.

William Roper House (above)

The first home to go up on East Battery, the Roper House was constructed in 1838 by cotton planter Robert William Roper. The three-story brick house was built on a grand scale with giant Ionic columns and arched terrace—an example of the Greek revival style popular in the 19th century.

Roper Harbor Views (opposite)

Built to take advantage of Charleston Harbor views, the Roper House boasts a five-columned portico, which sits about a ground-floor arcade of stuccoed brick. But the home didn't survive the Civil War completely unscathed; a 500-pound piece of a Confederate cannon has been in the attic since 1865.

Palmer House

Often referred to as the "Pink Palace," this home, built in 1848 by plantation owner John Ravenel, still remains in the family but has been a bed-and-breakfast since 1977. It sits on the only double lot on The Battery and boasts the city's first swimming pool and a large carriage house.

Pink House Gallery

Built in 1690, the charming Pink House on Chalmers Street is the oldest standing tavern building in the South. Today, it serves as an art gallery, specializing in landscapes, florals, Charleston scenes, and wildlife in both originals and fine art reproductions.

Aiken-Rhett House (top)

Built by Charleston merchant John Robinson and renovated by the Aiken family several times since 1827, when William Aiken, Sr. acquired it, the Aiken-Rhett House illustrates architectural trends during the first half of the 19th century, including late Federal period, Greek revival, and Victorian influences.

Hibiscus Bloom (left)

Beautiful and sometimes edible, many varietals of native hibiscus can be found all over Charleston, ranging from large shrubs to small trees that produce showy, colorful, trumpet-shaped flowers.

William Aiken House (opposite)

A popular venue for weddings and events in Charleston's Upper King Design District, the William Aiken House is named after its first owner. A National Historic Landmark, the property includes a pergola and reflection pool, along with two guest suites in a restored, Gothic-style carriage house.

Calhoun Mansion (*above*)

The largest residence in Charleston, the 24,000-square-foot Calhoun Mansion has 35 fireplaces, Japanese water gardens, a grand ballroom, private elevator, and a 90-foot-high cupola. Built in 1876 by George W. Williams, it also includes lighting designed and installed by Louis Comfort Tiffany.

Heyward-Washington House (*opposite*)

Located on Church Street in the downtown Historic District—within the original walled city—this brick home was built in 1772 by rice planter Daniel Heyward. The city rented it for George Washington during the president's weeklong visit in 1791; it is open for tours through the Charleston Museum.

Edward Rutledge House *(above)*

Famous for being the Charleston home of Edward Rutledge—lawyer, signer of the Declaration of Independence, politician, soldier, and governor of South Carolina—the large, nearly square building is a National Historic Landmark. The exterior has been left virtually untouched since it was built in 1787.

John Rutledge House *(opposite)*

John Rutledge, a signer of the Constitution of the United States, built this elegant home as a wedding gift for his bride, Elizabeth Grimke, in 1763. Now a bed-and-breakfast, the home features Italian marble fireplaces, parquet floors, and elaborate ironwork.

DeSaussure House *(above)*

The three-story stuccoed brick mansion built by auctioneer Louis D. DeSaussure between 1858 and 1861 is a prime example of antebellum architecture in The Battery neighborhood. Damaged and renovated after both the Civil War and the earthquake of 1886, it is currently divided into three residences.

Window Boxes *(left)*

Teal shutters set off beautiful window boxes, a common sight throughout downtown Charleston. Decorative and functional, shutters can be spotted on many of the city's historic homes.

Colonel John Stuart House *(opposite)*

Built by Colonel John Stuart in 1772, this three-story Georgian-style home on Tradd Street is distinctive, with a hipped roof, captain's walk, and narrow façade. It is the oldest surviving example of a side hall plan house in the city and features an elaborately carved wooden door surround.

Miles Brewton House

An excellent example of the "Charleston double house," the Miles Brewton House was designed by architect Ezra Waite. Built during 1765 to 1769, it is one of a few Palladian buildings in the South and was occupied as a military headquarters during the Revolutionary and Civil Wars.

Missroon House

Built in 1789, the Missroon House on East Bay Street was purchased in 1808 by Captain James Missroon, whose family owned it until after the Civil War. Currently it is the headquarters of the Historic Charleston Foundation, which aids in preserving Charleston's architectural history.

Window Boxes *(above)*

Fragrant Confederate jasmine climbs the shutters from the window boxes of this colorful home. The beautiful window boxes throughout downtown Charleston serve as an attractive welcome and give residents extra gardening space for historic homes that don't have large front yards.

Nathaniel Russell House *(opposite)*

This grand home-turned-museum on Meeting Street is one of America's most important neoclassical dwellings. Built by merchant Nathaniel Russell, it later served as a school for the Sisters of Charity of Our Lady of Mercy before being restored and opened for tours by the Historic Charleston Foundation.

Joseph Manigault House

Designed by architect Gabriel Manigault for his brother Joseph, this three-story brick townhouse is one of Charleston's best examples of federal architecture. Owned by the Charleston Museum, furnishings include American, English, and French pieces from the early 19th century.

Charles Pinckney House

The 28 acres of the Charleston Pinckney National Historic Site are a fraction of the large, 715-acre rice plantation Pinckney inherited from his father in 1782. This house was built of native cypress and pine in the 1820s and is an example of the tidewater cottages once common throughout the coastal Carolinas.

Battery Homes *(above and opposite)*

One of the most instantly recognizable portions of downtown Charleston, The Battery is a landmark defensive seawall and promenade. Named for a Civil War-era artillery battery at the site, it overlooks Charleston Harbor and boasts some of the city's most impressive and beautiful antebellum residences.

The Battery (above)

Created during the 1750s using boulders, stone, and masonry, The Battery seawall extends from the former Omar Shrine Temple to the intersection of Murray Boulevard and King Street. The stately homes along The Battery overlook landmarks including Fort Sumter, Castle Pinckney, the USS *Yorktown*, and more.

Battery Promenade (opposite, top and bottom)

At The Battery, visitors can admire—and touch—an impressive display of historic cannons and mortars that were used to defend the city during the Civil War. Palmetto trees and park benches sit parallel to the promenade, offering places to sit and admire the lower shores of the Charleston peninsula.

77

Edmonston-Alston House

General P. T. Beauregard watched the bombardment of Fort Sumter from the Edmonston-Alston House, the only house museum in the city with sweeping views of Charleston Harbor. Many of the Alston family's pieces remain in place, including family portraits and an original print of the Ordinance of Secession.

Battery House *(above and right)*

Although protected from the harbor by a seawall, homes along The Battery have been battered by hurricanes and earthquakes. "Earthquake bolts," black circles visible on the ends of several homes, are remnants of the Great Charleston Earthquake of 1886—the most destructive quake to strike east of the Mississippi.

French Huguenot Church *(above)*

Completed in 1845, this grand structure at the corner of Church and Queen streets, is the oldest Gothic Revival church in South Carolina and contains the oldest church organ in the city—a pipe organ made by Henry Erben of New York.

St. Philip's Episcopal Church *(opposite)*

The beautiful St. Philip's Episcopal Church stands watch over Church Street, topped by a 210-foot steeple. The church's cemetery is the final resting place of many notable Charlestonians, including John C. Calhoun, who served as vice president under John Quincy Adams and General Andrew Jackson.

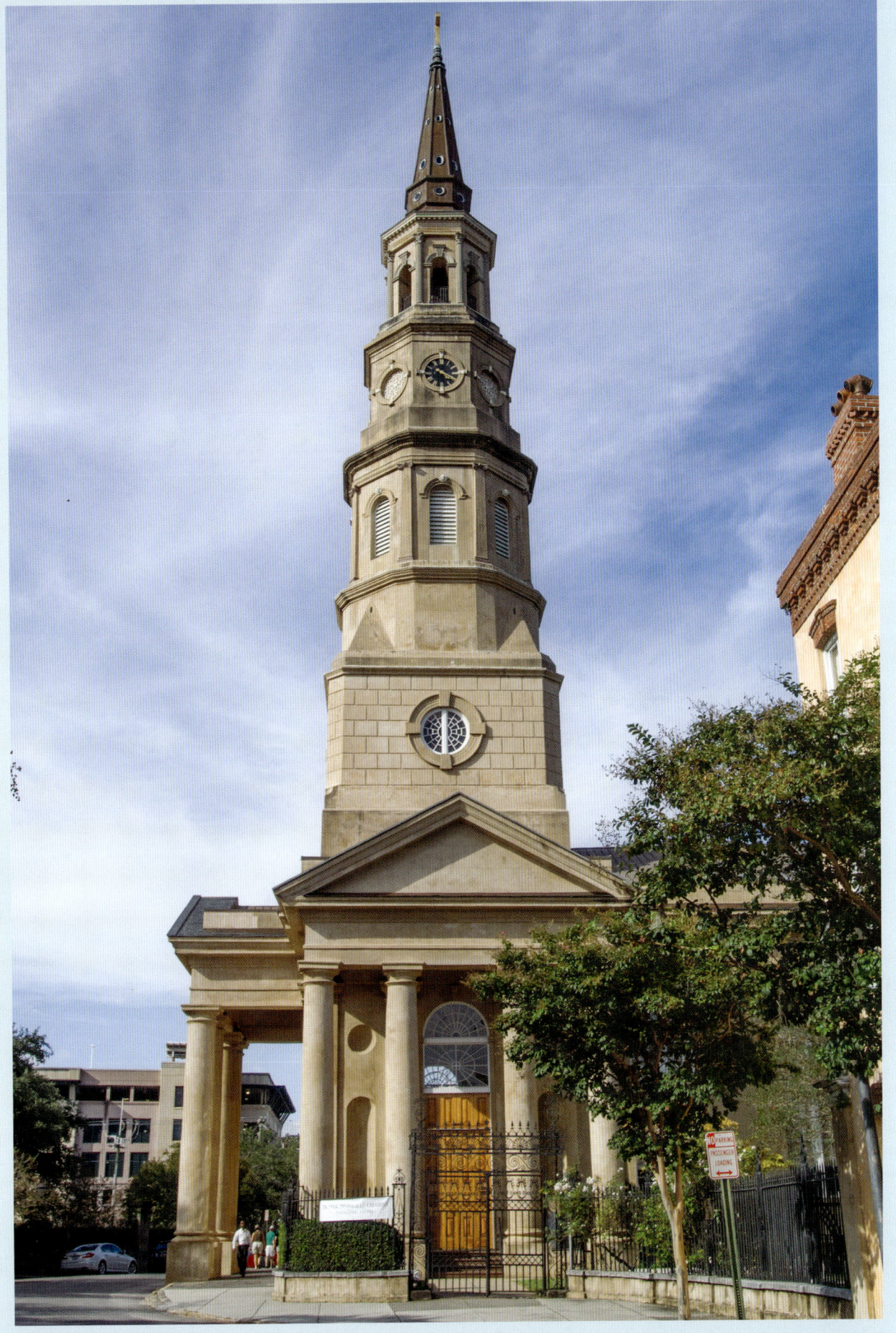

St. Michael's Episcopal Church

The oldest church structure in Charleston, St. Michael's Episcopal boasts a 186-foot-high steeple. The clock, imported from England in 1764, originally had just an hour hand for each face—minute hands were added in 1849. It is the oldest functioning colonial tower clock in the United States.

St. Mary's of the Annunciation

Established in 1789, St. Mary's was the first Catholic church in the Carolinas. The church register was kept in French until 1822—and in the church's crowded graveyard, inscriptions are written in Latin, French, and English, representing seventeen nationalities across two centuries and three continents.

Cathedral of St. John the Baptist *(opposite)*

Built on the foundation of the original 1854 cathedral, which burned in 1861, the Cathedral of St. John the Baptist is made from Connecticut tool-chiseled brownstone. The spire was included in the original plans, but a lack of funding meant it wasn't completed for another 103 years.

Unitarian Church *(above)*

In a city with an abundance of magnificent churches—and the nickname the "Holy City"—it can be overwhelming to take them all in. But the Unitarian Church, with its spectacular fan-vaulted ceiling and painted glass window, is considered among the finest in the country and should not be missed.

A Day in the Life *(above)*

Modern life mixes with history every day on the streets of Charleston—including here, on Queen Street, where a bike and parking meter sit in front of contemporary art gallery and boutique LimeBlue.

Central Station *(opposite)*

The iron pavilion at this double fire station, the largest of three stations built following the city's devastating 1886 earthquake, was built on the site of an 1847 artesian well. It includes monuments to fallen Charleston firefighters and the bell from the Cannon Street Station watchtower.

F.V.F.D
PROTECTION

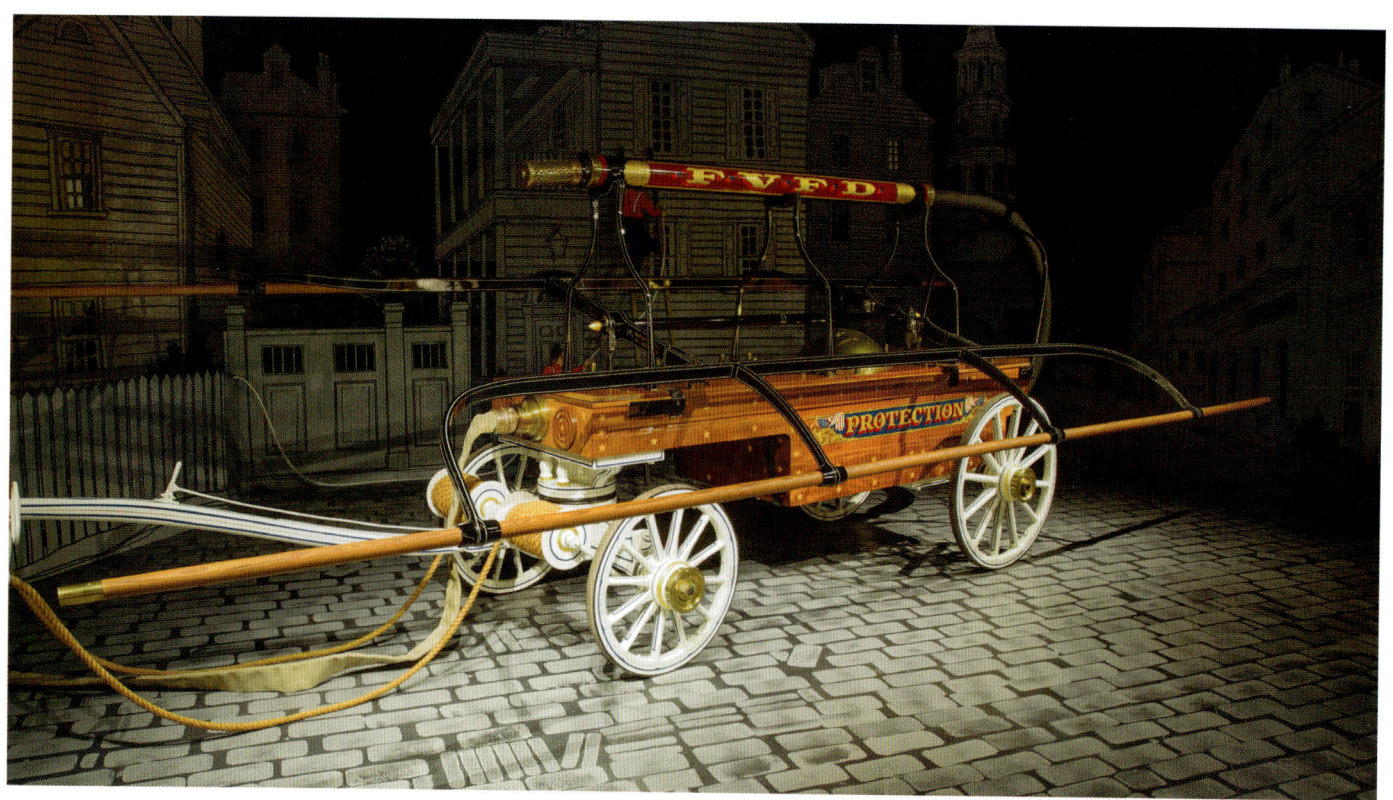

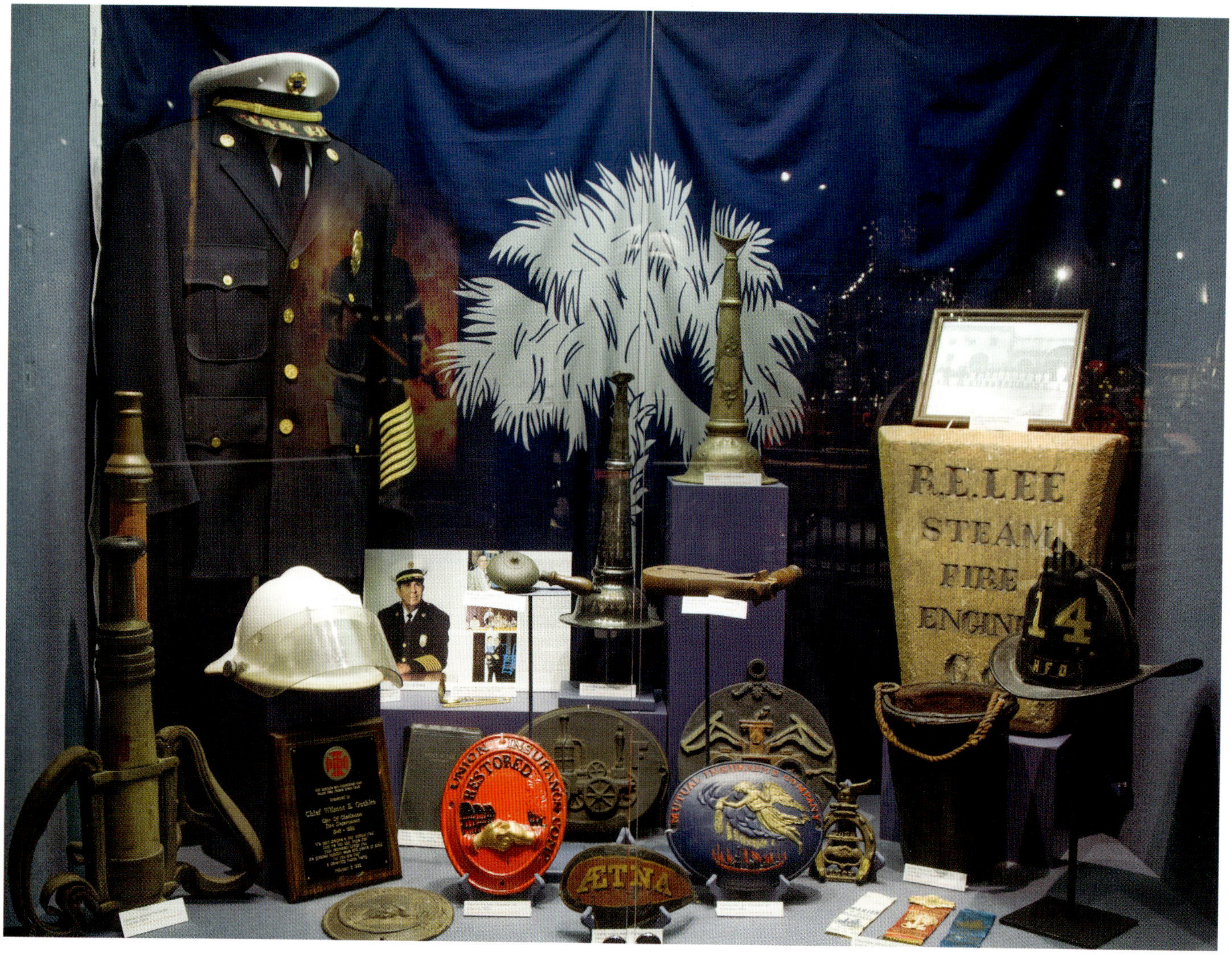
R.E.LEE
STEAM
FIRE
14
RESTORED
ÆTNA

Fire Museum and Education Center *(opposite, top and bottom)*

The 26,000-square-foot North Charleston and American LaFrance Fire Museum and Education Center offers visitors a glimpse into the life of a firefighter across the centuries—from antique fire equipment to interactive displays and a fire truck simulator.

Restored Fire Equipment *(above)*

The museum houses the largest collection of professionally restored American LaFrance fire equipment in the nation, including a collection of 18 fully restored vehicles dating to the early 1800s and valued at nearly $5 million. All of the restored vehicles are in working condition.

Gibbes Museum of Art

A horse-drawn carriage tour passes the Gibbes Museum of Art, named for James Schoolbred Gibbes, Sr. Established in 1858 by the Carolina Art Association, it moved to its present location in 1905 and houses artwork from the 18th century to present, in addition to being a popular wedding and events venue.

South Carolina Historical Society

Housed in the historic Robert Mills Fireproof Building on Meeting Street, the South Carolina Historical Society was formed in 1855 to preserve the state's historical resources. The Palladian-style, three-story building is the first fireproof structure in the United States built specifically to protect documents.

South Carolina Aquarium *(top and bottom)*

The South Carolina Aquarium opened in 2000 with a mission of educating visitors and conserving the aquatic environments of the state. Jutting 200 feet into Charleston Harbor, the 93,000-square-foot aquarium's nine galleries explore the state's aquatic environments from the ocean to the mountains.

The Great Ocean Tank *(opposite)*

The centerpiece of the aquarium is a two-story, 385,000-gallon ocean tank, home to the 220-pound loggerhead sea turtle, Caretta, in addition to more than 5,000 aquatic animals, from river otters and sharks to American alligators. Divers interact with visitors during daily dive shows.

Manicured Gardens *(opposite)*

Magnolia Plantation's beautiful gardens, the oldest unrestored gardens in America, have drawn admiration since they first opened in 1870. The gardens are known for their large collections of camellia and azalea, as well as the iconic white bridge —a favorite stop for photographs.

Magnolia Plantation *(above)*

Ten rooms of the Drayton home are open to the public at Magnolia Plantation, offering a glimpse into plantation life in the early 19th century. The core of the home was built prior to the Revolutionary War near Summerville and floated down the Ashley River to the plantation after the Civil War.

Audubon Swamp Garden *(right)*

The garden is named for John James Audubon, the famous naturalist and hunter known for his bird paintings, who was once a guest of Magnolia Plantation. A favorite destination for wildlife enthusiasts, the swamp can be accessed without a general admission ticket.

Beautiful Wetlands *(top and bottom)*

In the 60-acre blackwater swamp, thousands of plant and animal species can be found among the hauntingly beautiful cypress and tupelo trees. The Audubon Swamp Garden is a thriving natural environment and home to many varieties of mammals, birds, and reptiles, from bald eagles to otters, turtles, and alligators.

Exploring the Swamp *(above)*

Birding and photography are popular activities here, and it's easy to see why. Exploring the landscape by boardwalk, bridge, and dike, visitors can spot egrets, herons, and other waterfowl, which nest within feet of the path. For a different point of view, nature boat tours take visitors through old rice fields.

Audubon Swamp Garden *(pages 98 – 99)*

Originally used as a freshwater reservoir for Magnolia Plantation's rice fields, the swamp is now a wetland habitat traversed by trails, boardwalks, and bridges. The flooded forests are home to slow-growing bald cypress trees, which can live for more than 1,000 years and reach heights of up to 150 feet.

Reflections at Middleton Place *(above)*

A blaze of azaleas reflects on the water at Middleton Place, America's oldest landscaped gardens, which begun in 1741 and reflect the grand, classical garden design fashionable in Europe and England in the 18th century. Geometry, balance, beautiful vistas, and focal points are the hallmarks of the garden.

Middleton Place *(opposite)*

Exploring the original gardens at Middleton Place is a pleasure for the senses, especially when the azaleas are in full bloom—there are many beautiful allées in which trees and shrubs are planted to appear as walls that partition off segments of the garden.

Beautiful Vistas *(above and opposite)*

Majestic, Spanish moss-draped trees stand guard along the water at Middleton Place. Growing throughout the Lowcountry, the silvery-gray plant isn't actually a moss—it's a bromeliad, a flowering plant commonly found on the southern live oak or bald cypress. Native Americans called it "tree hair."

Middleton Place *(pages 104 – 105)*

It reportedly took 100 slaves nearly a decade to complete the walks, artificial lakes, and vistas like this hillside. The gardens fell into neglect after the Civil War, but J. J. Pringle Smith, a Middleton descendent, completed a 15-year restoration project before opening the gardens to the public year-round in 1952.

White Point Gardens *(above and left)*

Created as a public garden in 1837, this prominent landmark at the point of the Charleston peninsula is a beautiful setting to take in Charleston Harbor views. Many graceful statues and fountains can be found here, including the Fort Moultrie Monument, featuring a statue of Revolutionary War hero Sergeant William Jasper.

Little Dancer *(opposite)*

Little Dancer, commissioned in 1962 by Sally Carrington was created by Charleston sculptor Willard Hirsch and installed as a water fountain in White Point Garden. Hirsch had created the original model for this sculpture in the 1940s. Today, more than 20 castings can be found throughout the country.

Bandstand *(top and bottom)*

Built in 1907 as a memorial from Martha W. Carrington to her mother, the original owners of the Calhoun Mansion, the Williams Music Pavilion is surrounded by a canopy of live oak. Although amplified concerts have been outlawed, it is a popular location for weddings and special events.

Beauty at White Point

The majestic beauty of White Point Garden belies its sometimes-unsavory past. In 1718, infamous—and not particularly successful—"gentleman pirate" Stede Bonnet was hanged here with several other pirates. He was buried in the nearby marsh; his epitaph stands in the park today.

Magnolia Cemetery *(above and left)*

The oldest public cemetery in Charleston opened in 1850 on the site of Magnolia Umbra Rice Plantation. Still in use today, it is the final resting place of many prominent South Carolinians and considered one of the best examples of Victorian cemetery design in the United States.

William Burroughs Smith Grave *(opposite)*

Named "the richest man in Charleston" in his 1892 obituary in *The State*, the pyramid-shaped monument at Magnolia Cemetery marks the grave of W. B. Smith. Governors Thomas Bennett, Langdon Cheves, Horace L. Huntley, and Robert Barnwell Rhett are also buried here.

The Charleston Museum

"America's first museum," the Charleston Museum was founded in 1773, when South Carolina was a British colony. Here, visitors can admire permanent exhibits including some of the earliest known artifacts from the settlement of Charles Towne, along with a roster of rotating exhibits from the archives.

Circular Congregational Church (opposite)

Founded in 1681, the unusual Circular Congregational Church boasts one of the oldest continuously worshiping congregations in the South, and its graveyard is the city's oldest. Shaped by its independent members, the church often was the meeting place for supporters of political and religious freedom.

Second Presbyterian Church (above)

Organized in 1809 and dedicated in 1811, the Second Presbyterian Church on Meeting Street was built outside then-city limits at a cost of $100,000. It is the fourth oldest church structure in the city, and gave its church bell to the Confederacy in 1862 to be turned into cannon metal.

Old Slave Mart Museum *(opposite)*

Once called "the shed" and the home of Charleston's slave auctions, the museum now shares the story of the city's role in inter-state slave trade. Formerly part of a complex known as Ryan's Mart, it is the last remaining building used as a slave auction gallery in South Carolina.

Powder Magazine *(above)*

The Powder Magazine, built in 1713 to store the city's gunpowder supply, is the oldest public building in the state. Designed with 32-inch walls and a hip roof, the building was constructed to implode if an explosion was to occur inside the building.

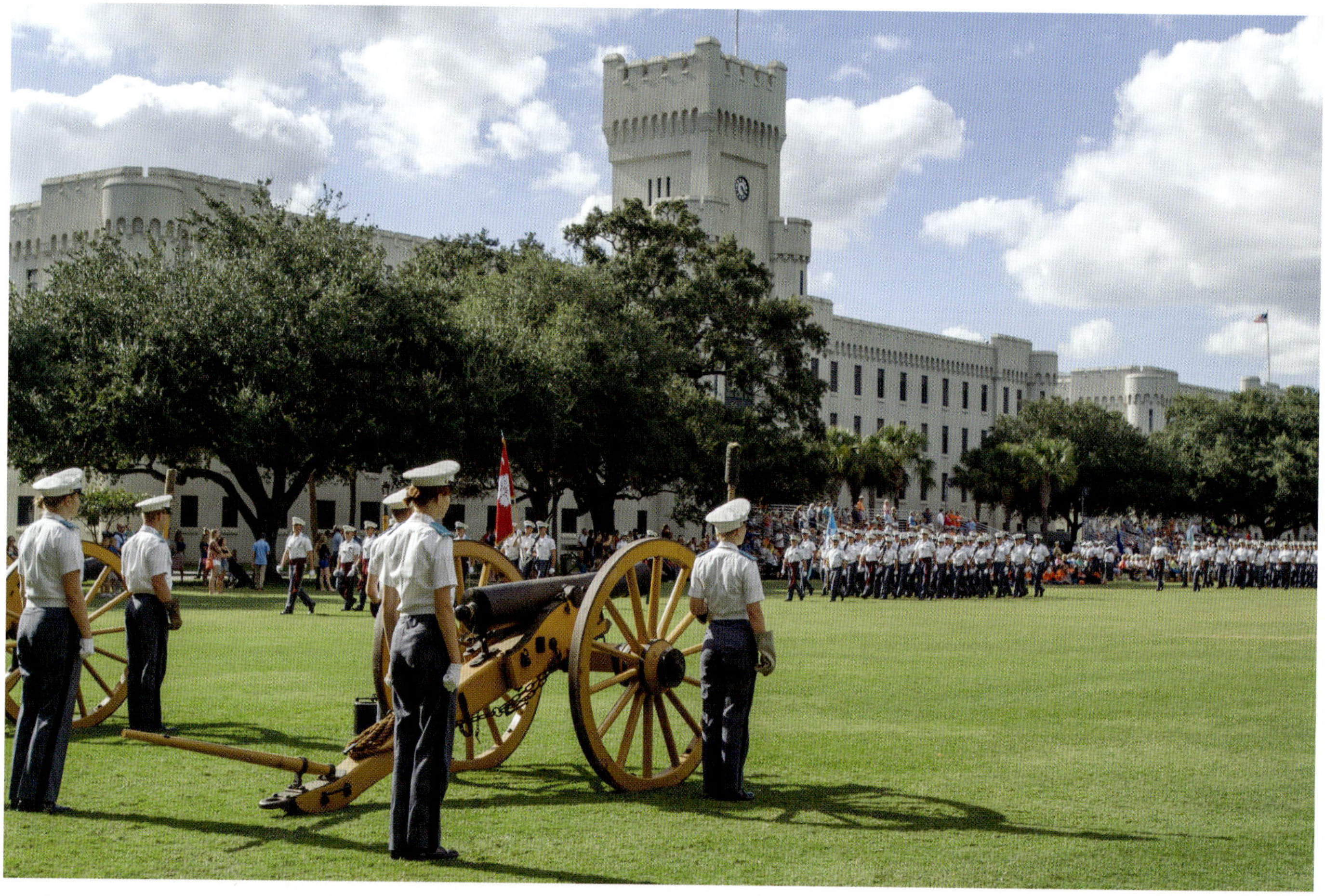

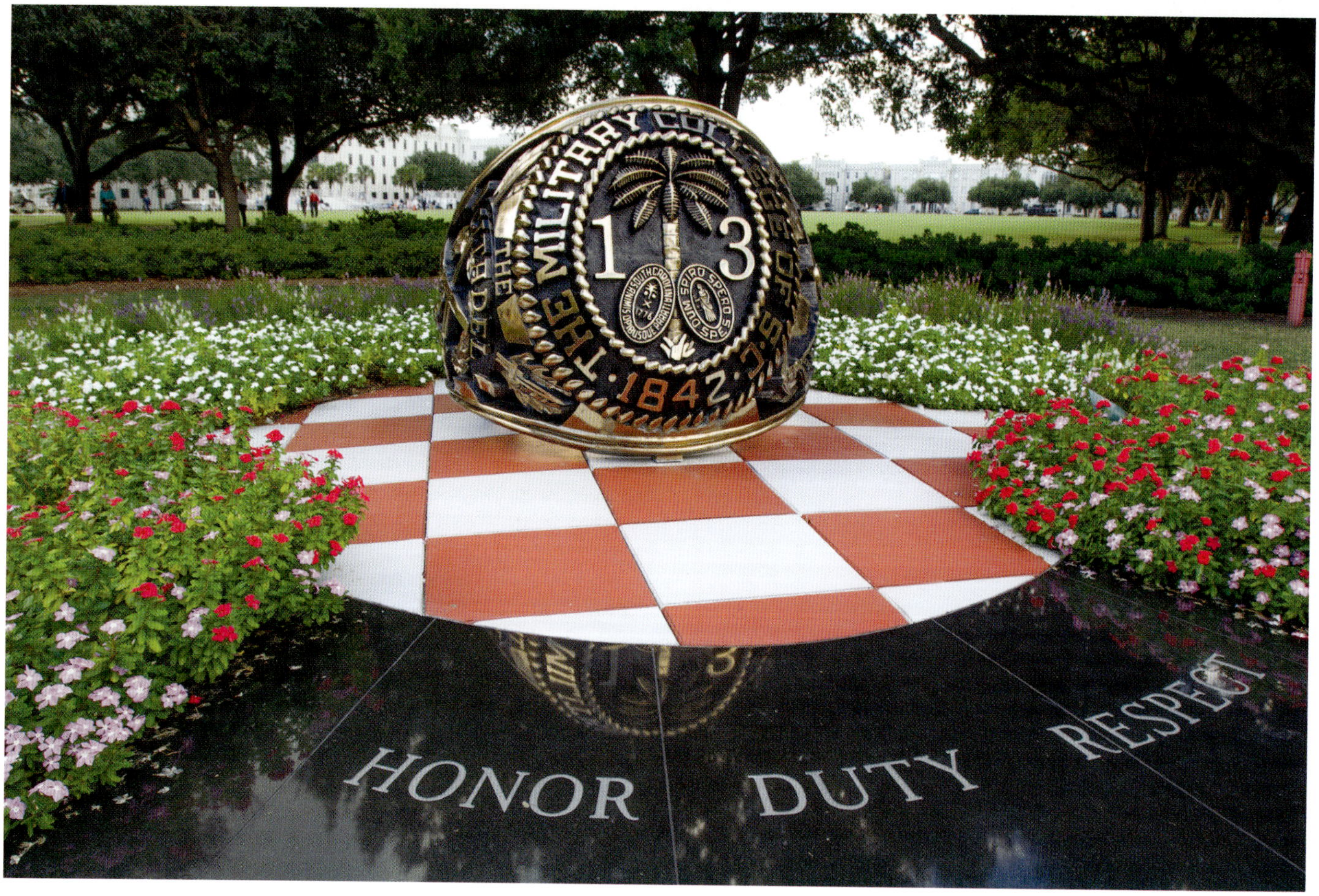
THE MILITARY
1 3
1842
HONOR
DUTY
RESPECT

The Citadel *(opposite, top)*

The Military College of South Carolina, commonly called The Citadel, was founded in 1842. With an undergraduate student body of about 2,000 cadets, today it sits on 300 acres along the Ashley River, with a complex of buildings surrounding a 10-acre grass parade ground.

Citadel Ring Statue *(opposite, bottom)*

Located at the gateway to The Citadel campus, the Citadel Ring Statue celebrates the military college's core values: duty, honor, and respect. Each year the interchangeable numbers on the crest of the ring are changed to represent the most recent class to receive class rings.

The Old Citadel *(above)*

The Citadel was originally located on what is now Marion Square, in a Romanesque building designed by Charleston architect Frederick Wesner to serve as the South Carolina State Arsenal. Classes were held here from 1842 to 1922, when the campus moved to its current location. Today, the building is a hotel.

Charleston Southern University

One of the state's largest independent universities with more than 3,200 students, Charleston Southern University in North Charleston sits on 300 acres that were formerly a rice and indigo plantation. Founded in 1964, it is affiliated with the South Carolina Baptist Convention.

Lightsey Chapel Auditorium

The Lightsey Chapel Auditorium is a reflection of the school's commitment to integrating faith and education. Named for W. Norris and Nell Peeples Lightsey, it is the university's home for concerts, theatre, worship, and other events.

College of Charleston *(above and opposite)*

Majestic Randolph Hall is the centerpiece of the College of Charleston's campus, founded in 1770. Named for Harrison Randolph, the college's 11th president, it was completed in 1829 and is one of the oldest college buildings in the country that is still in use.

Cooper River (above)

An aerial view of the Charleston peninsula and Cooper River offers a birds-eye view of the Arthur Ravenel Jr. Bridge. Built at a cost of $632 million, the cable-stayed bridge has 128 individual cables; each of the bridge's towers reaches a height of 572.5 feet, making them the tallest structures in the state.

Cooper River Bridge Run
(opposite, top and bottom)

First held in 1978, the Cooper River Bridge Run, a competitive 10K run, begins in Mount Pleasant, crosses the Ravenel Bridge, and finishes in downtown Charleston. This signature event draws runners from around the world and includes a three-day festival.

127

Photo by William Struhs

A native Charlestonian, **Rick Rhodes** discovered a passion for photography at an early age. His interest led him to study at The Southeast Center for Photographic Studies in Daytona Beach, Florida and then to Brooks Institute of Photography in Santa Barbara, California. Returning to his beloved Charleston, he focuses on commercial photography and fine art reproduction. He enjoys aerial, architectural, and landscape photography. Rick's expertise has allowed him to work with numerous local and national clients.

Rick works out of his studio in Charleston, South Carolina. He also teaches at two local colleges, serves on the board of The American Society of Media Photographers, and leads music at his church.

Rick's passion for photography has grown far beyond just the photographic process. The whole experience has enhanced his journey in which he has never stopped believing. You can see more of his work at www.rickrhodesphotography.com.

Aleigh Acerni is a Charlotte, N.C.-based writer, editor, and author. She has been an editor at award-winning publications including *skirt!*, *Where* magazine, and *Charlotte* magazine. She is especially drawn to writing about food, travel, natural beauty, sustainability, gardening, and green living. She is the co-author of *Justice at Guantanamo: One Woman's Odyssey and Her Crusade for Human Rights*, with attorney Kristine Huskey, published by Globe Pequot Press in 2009. Find her online at www.aleighacerni.com.